INCONSOLABLE OBJECTS

Inconso

Nancy Miller Gomez

lable
Objects

YESYES BOOKS *Portland*

Cover Design: Alban Fischer
Interior Design: KMA Sullivan
Cover Art: "Owl Collage" by Alexandra Gallagher
Author Photo Credit: Chris Schmauch
Project Lead: Gale Marie Thompson

ISBN 978-1-936919-97-0
Printed in the United States of America

Published by YesYes Books
1631 NE Broadway St #121
Portland, OR 97232
yesyesbooks.com

KMA Sullivan, Publisher
Devin Devine, Assistant Editor
Alban Fischer, Graphic Designer
Karah Kemmerly, Mananging Editor
Jill Kolongowski, Manuscript Copy Editor
James Sullivan, Assistant Editor
Gale Marie Thompson, Senior Editor, Book Development

Contents

For Arrow, Atlas, Deven, Dylan, Edan, Joel, Jonah,
Julian, Lindsay, Maya, Mitch, and Tamara
—*The Brilliant Galaxy Around Which My Life Revolves.*

In memory of Blanche and Herb. For Tom. For Babette.

I

Snapshot

I was a hand grenade of a girl
vacuum packed into a dress

that bound my body
like a bandage staunching a wound.

My arms were cinched in tourniquets
of tulle, my throat choked in a rage

of lace. I'd hacked my hair into chaos.
Kept it ragged and short. Kept my fists

clenched in the fuselage of my lap. My eyes —
two foxholes. No light escaped. My lips

stretched across my face like a trip wire.
The man with the camera said, *you can do better.*

Give me a smile. I set my mouth
into the look I've kept all these years.

That's still me in the photo,
waiting to pull the pin.

Tilt-A-Whirl

It was a hot day in Paola, Kansas.
       The rides were banging around empty

as we moved through the carnival music and catcalls.
       At the Tilt-A-Whirl we were the only ones.

My big sister chose our carriage carefully,
       walking a full circle until she stopped.

The ride operator didn't take his eyes off her
       long dark hair and amber eyes, ringed

like the golden interior of a newly felled pine.
       She didn't seem to notice him lingering

as he checked the lap bar and my sister asked
       in her sweetest, most innocent — or maybe

not-so-innocent — voice, *Can we have a long ride*
       please, mister? When he sat back down

at the joystick, he made a show
       of lighting his smoke while the cage

of his face settled into a smile
       I would one day learn to recognize,

and then those dizzying red teacups began to spin
        my sister and me into woozy amusement.

We forgot the man, the heat, our thighs
        sticking to the vinyl seats, our bodies glued

together in a centrifugal blur of happiness
        beneath a red metal canopy

as we picked up speed and started to laugh,
        our heads thrown back, mouths open,

the fabric of my sister's shirt clinging
        to the swinging globes of her breasts

as we went faster, and faster,
        though we had begun to scream *Stop!*

Please stop! Until our voices grew hoarse
        beneath the clattering pivots and dips,

the air filling with diesel and cigarettes, and the man
        at the control stick, waiting for us

to spin toward him again, and each time he cocked his hand
as if sighting prey down the barrel of a gun.

Bust

I saw the angel in the marble and carved until I set him free.
—MICHELANGELO

All through that long, hot summer,
the tap, tap, tap of my father's hammer
filled the house. *Sit still,*

my mother said, *or he won't
get your features right.* But already
the dark seam had appeared,

and every strike of the tooth chisel,
the rasp, the gouging tool,
revealed only more darkness

as the shadow spread across
the alabaster that was becoming
my face. To dig out the flaws,

my father sliced through crystal
and calcite, milked the bones
until his fingers bled. He carved

with his teeth and his tongue,
gnawed the cold stone until
his jaws ached and his eyes wept

white dust. But it was not possible
to carve out the streaks of night
unsheathed on my cheek.

And me, laboring to sit still, twisting
and turning, as something that wasn't
an angel rose to the surface.

Coachwhip

It was the winter the snake went missing.
We searched through laundry hampers,
peered into toilets, stepped everywhere
carefully. No one slept well.

On the eve of the eighth day,
my mother turned on the garbage disposal
and heard the gargle of blades
grinding through bones and flesh. Later,

she fished out the mangled creature
with an oven mitt and laid it down
outside on a bed of snow-capped compost.
All that year I dreamt of knives

sleeping beneath me. Mornings,
I woke to the memory
of the beautiful black coils,
the diamond-braided skin in ribbons.

And because I was a child
plagued by imagination, I waited
for them to rise up from the drain,
silent as shadows,

the kitchen brimming with generations
of snakes draped over the chairs
and light fixtures, a river
of lacerated bodies slithering out of the sink,

while the largest serpent slipped off,
tasting the air with his tongue,
sidewinding down the hall
in search of my mother.

Talking to the Tornado

It wasn't into the howl
of wind or the screaming of trees
uprooting themselves. It wasn't into
the metal shriek of the double wide
tumbling down the street, dragging
its own clothesline still flying
one white nightie
in surrender.

Not into the groan
of the barn giving way, shingles
popping off like plucked feathers,
or into the last gasp
of row homes collapsing,
the swings in a frenzy
on the empty play yard.

It was into the silence.

Into the quiet that paced like a feral cat
around the storm, an eerie stillness
that hotwired every inhale,
and made the hair on my arms stand up
and dance.

Into that hush my father spoke,

coaxing the sky to uncoil,
to lift one hungry finger
into its dark mouth,
and taste the peace offering
of a madman.

My father, holding his hands before him
in supplication — as if placating a troubled child,
his face a beacon of calm,

one human with his own lonely demons
offering consolation as my mother
and older siblings huddled
in the basement while I hid outside
to watch my father commune
with the delirious world.

I'll never know
what secrets the wind told my father
or the strange language he spoke,
coaxing it to put down its wrath,
pick its way around the lake,
and wander off
in a different direction.

Kansas

I've heard it said, *Youth is nothing*
but sadness and longing,
but whatever sadness there was
has followed me to this place where I am lonely

for a two-lane highway stretching out
behind me in the rearview mirror
of an orange Opal GT, the car
I eased out of the garage for joyrides
long before I could legally drive.

I'm lonely for the rows of tract homes
that cropped up like winter wheat.

For basements smelling of damp cement
and secrets. Leaf piles and bonfires,
the air throbbing with the metallic whine
and clicks of cicadas and katydids.

I miss fish-eyed skies drenched
in dry lightning. Candle flies
and June bugs, their gangly legs trapped
in the screen door, my sister screeching
when they snared in her curly hair.

I even miss the bagworms my father paid us to pick
from the pine trees all fall, slimy creatures
that looked like tiny green penises
sliding out from their shaggy sheath of needles.

I miss the *tsssk* of lawn sprinklers
and redbuds reaching for one another
above a fallen fence.

For the muddy taste of channel cats.
Soaked in buttermilk, dredged in flour,
dropped into cast iron spitting with hot fat.

For tubular hay bales, and wind-tossed fields
of purple alfalfa. For the smell
of horseshit and the ancient attic fan
that filled our house with a hot wind
and a roaring hum
as if each night we'd bedded down
in the purling throat of God. I'm lonely

for the safe feeling
of sleeping next to my sister,
our beds shoved together, books
piled across the window seat
looking over the lake. I'm lonely
for the smell of lake. From here,
I can barely see
the dock, softly rocking.

Resurrection

When I was five my brother convinced me
          to perform mouth to mouth on a catfish
floating belly up in the scum that gathered
          in the lake behind our house. He said I had the power

to bring it back, though it was my choice.
          I followed his directions, leaned over the dock,
pressed my lips against the stiff ridge of its mouth
          (while keeping its bloated body submerged

beneath the oily sheen) and began to breathe in
          and out as I opened and closed the bony folds
of its gills. At first, my brother held my ankles, to steady me
          so I wouldn't fall off the dock. I kept breathing

in through my nose — sting of creosote and pond rot —
          and out through my mouth — a soft exhale of prayer.
You already know I did not bring the fish back to life,
          though it wasn't for lack of trying. I kept breathing

into that dark opening long after my brother said to quit,
          long after he got bored and wandered off,
and the setting sun bathed the brackish water in gold.
          I kept breathing in and out, long after the night cooled,

and the stars rose, and my mother found me asleep
　　　on the dock, her voice calling me back from that place,
where the fish turned its rapturous eyes away from the moon,
　　　and dove back to its sanctuary of darkness.

The Invisible Mother

. . . in the Victorian era . . . young children were photographed with their mother present but hidden . . . —WIKIPEDIA

The mother-shape draped in dark cloth
takes on the properties of a chair, a curtain,
a cloak. She becomes a living field of fabric,

a blank screen. An erasure. Lint gathers
in her eyes and the corners of her mouth.
She is the rustling in the room,

the empty place where dust gathers.
Her heart is made of cobwebs, her words
glued to the roof of her mouth. No one sees her

chin quivering like a small bird. She has folded
her sorrows into napkins placed at a table
set for her children. They feast until nothing is left

but her absence. Her fingers tap out time,
measuring seconds. She is a forgotten thought,
a lamp, a stage, a station of the cross. She bears it

silently, this weight, her babies propped across
her motionless body. She wears the finery
of their bones to mask her naked face.

She is counterbalance, stanchion, a breathing
pillar of brocade. The space where she begins
and ends debated endlessly in velvet.

Missing History

Researchers have estimated that women's stories make up just 0.5 percent of recorded history. —THE NEW YORK TIMES

Look in the graveyard.
Look under the bed.

Look in the woods.
In the barn. In the box

where my grandmother
kept her life's work.

After she died,
her manuscripts vanished.

Look in the mirror
Look in the empty cup.

Look in the night,
where the matriarchs seed your dreams,

or in the mud hut
where words mix with menstrual blood.

Look in the weave of the blanket,
the tensed warp of tapestries,
the pottery stained with ochre and loss.

Sometimes I feel my grandmother,
a canary, stilled in my throat.
A smolder of story

I'm trying to revive.

In the unsung hum I hear
her lips pressed silent.

Look under the leaves and rocks.
Inside the cage of my ribs.

Look in the river.

My granddaughter singing to herself
in wings and birdsong.
Her bloodline burning.

Look in the fire.

How to Forget

I am lining my memories up against the wall.
They are begging me for reprieve. Here is the night
I found you on the floor, folded

like laundry. Here are the bloody towels,
the smell of ammonia and rotting fruit.
Once I was a wife. Now

I am a wilderness. I am the grove
of aspens. All that's left of you
are candle stubs and carpet stains.

All your goodbyes have turned into horses.
They are grazing peacefully. Your words
are blades of grass, our last argument

a pasture dotted with poppies.
That night I watched you wash
your bruised hands in the sink. Now,

I see two fish diving into a stream.
I am re-remembering the last time
we spoke. I have turned it into a holiday,

marked it on the calendar
with an asterisk. A day to eat cake.
A day to enter the cellar

and retrieve the special vintage
with its sweet notes of smoke and honey.
Lush on the tongue. Easy to swallow.

The golden crowned sparrows
have returned from their long summer
singing of loss. Three notes.

One for the knife, one for the cut,
one for all I have
forgotten.

Crescent Moon

You died the year our youngest son turned one.
Eyes closed, mouth slack, hair splayed
around your face like an electric fence,
a rusty crown on an otherworldly prince.

It was the final affront, an end
to the prolonged "fuck you" of your short life —
leaving all those promises you made eternally unfulfilled,
and me with two children tethered
to the unsteady buoy of my heart, all of us holding on
for dear life, riding out the riptides
of utility bills and rent and getting food on the table.

I'm still emptying the dumpster of our years together.
Old hypodermics and broken bottles,
shoeboxes filled with notebooks and guitar picks.

I'm still finding the landmines you left.
Like today, when our daughter turned her head
and I saw the dimple that used to bloom
in a crescent moon on the right side of your smile,
and all that love came rushing back.

I remember
those years when you were still alive
and always around
to haunt us.

We All Fall Down

Ashes coated my son's cheeks,
his lashes, his hands still gripping
the pressure-sealed bag
that exploded when he opened it.
I just wanted to see, he said.
I wiped soot off his eyebrows,
rubbed a smudge above his lip.
It came out everywhere, he said,
and we both began to laugh,
gasps that grew into a keening
and filled the room.
Then we were silent.
I helped my son sweep his dad
off the chairs, the stairs, emptied
the inside of his shoes and collar,
but the gritty gray bits
of bone and ash wouldn't fit
back inside the plastic urn.
Could it be, even after death,
love expands? We scooped up
what was left and dropped it
from the balcony
like snow.

Mothering

No patter of tender words.
No swaddle and coo swing.
Just escape routes and safety gates.

A nest galvanized in devotion.
Tempered in blood and hunger.
No cushion. No cradle.

A rusty, war-weary, single-mothership
carved of teeth and tenacity.
No bassinet, no bumpers. A flesh-bed

lined with fur ripped from her
own limbs. No rock-a-bye, no pat-a-cake.
A howl, a bay, a euphoric barking.

No cosset, no coddle, only this
guard-dog of body,
the cow-bellowing huntress

crouched and kill-ready.
She feeds her daughter books
chewed to word-pulp, offers wisdom

from her weeping breasts,
lessons leached from her
work-worn fingers. She will raise

no pussy-willowed, kitten thing.
She abides no lanyard making,
gods-eye crafting princess school

of nail polish and baked goods.
No ruffles. No frills. Nothing pinked
or plucked smooth. No picket fence,

no flower box. Just safe house
and shield-maiden. Just spine
and grindstone. Her drawbridge-eyes

always watching what she begat.
Night-minder. Mercenary.
All those stone-broke years.

She-wolf. Always predator. Never Prey.
Her heart winterized, her throat
ripped in battle chant. And when

the child's ready, she bites,
and claws and storms her way
into the world.

No barbed wire, no border,
no palisade will hold the girl
this terrible love hath wrought.

How Are We Doing?

The man working window eleven
at the DMV wears a happy face
pinned to his nametag as if he's hosting
a social event. But even from here,

three people back, I can see
Frank is having a bad day.
He keeps tapping the same key,
hoping the computer will do something different.

Poor Frank tapping harder and harder,
pausing sometimes to stare owl-eyed
at a young woman waving her paperwork
as if she's trying to reignite

a dying fire. Her pretty face has grown ugly
in anger. She smacks the counter, demanding
to know the problem. Roused from her desk,
a grenade-shaped woman drifts over

to hover above Frank. She gives him directions
in a tight, managerial voice (so unmusical,
you'd call it noise) while Frank continues to tap
and tap until she commandeers his keyboard,

fixes the issue and walks off, leaving the stamping
and stapling to Frank, who hustles with a deference
that hurts to watch. Meanwhile the man in front of me
has given up and huffed out of the building.

But Frank, I want to lean over the counter
into your small, personal space and straighten
your reading glasses that have gone askew.
Their broken frames hang cockeyed

off the thin bridge of your nose
like pipe cleaners in a preschool project.
I want to batten down that piece of your hair
sticking up. Except I'm still in a line

that isn't moving, and I fear the office will close
before I've had a chance to tell you
how sorry I am that life has brought you here
to this place where all these people

unwind like a frayed rope
into the unhappy well of your workdays.
But finally, it's my turn, Frank,
to look you in the eyes and ask you

to process my papers. How hard is it, really,
to notice the way you bunch one corner
of your mouth into a half-smile or blink
at the mention of your name,

a name I have carried in my heart
for all of these twenty minutes.
So when you hand me back
my temporary license, along with a form

that asks, *How are we doing?*
I want to believe there is someone
watching over us to whom I can respond,
Please, we're not doing well here.

The doors to the building have been locked.
The office is empty.
We are lonely and hurting,
and night has just begun.

The Road

*— Farther up the road lay a heart without a body. It was unclear
from which soldier it had come. (Last line of an article in the* LOS ANGELES
TIMES *about the Russian invasion of Ukraine, March 5, 2022.)*

There was a dead man lying face down in the road.
For days, his body lay in the snow. And the soldiers who saw it
felt a wintery stillness move through them. They paused

to regard the afternoon shadows and then kept on with their marching.
The men stepped carefully around a torso —
its arms stretched out like a swan landing on water,

what used to be legs twisted like a broken ladder.
They were following orders. When the men marched by the heart
they thought they could hear the sound of it

no longer beating, a deep silence that rose
through the soles of their boots and seemed to grow
out of the ground they walked on. The men clutched their guns

to their chests. They had thought to fight a war
and be done with it. But a heart lay in the road.
And they will never stop hearing the sound of it

not beating. They will carry it back to their families.
They will hear it while singing their children to sleep.
They will lay down with the emptiness and wake in the night listening

to what isn't there. The road will never go back to being a road,
or the field a field. The earth will gather up the silence and play it
in graveyards and grasslands. And on either side of the road

that is no longer just a road, where wild cherry trees stand vigil,
their branches crusted with ice. The land will go on mourning,
and the trees will burst with fruit the color of fresh blood.

Men die for that sweetness.

Red-Winged Blackbirds

Pint-sized dive-bombers.
We wore pans on our heads
to get near the plum tree. The ring
of beaks hitting metal thrilled us.
We were delirious with fear.
The fruit stained our mouths
the color of blood. It tasted dangerous.
How I hungered for it.

Siren Song

A songbird mimicking the sounds of emergency sirens has been caught on video . . . —CNN

A starling has taught himself to sing
like an ambulance. Now the air is filled

with emergencies. *Whee-o, whee-o,* high and low,
a fire truck rides out of a mockingbird's mouth.

Grackles impersonate police cars. They dive-bomb
the precinct parking lot, bashing their beaks

into the side-view mirrors of their rivals.
The magpie knows a lovely air raid. Now

she trills like a helicopter, next a chain saw,
then an AK47. The quail stop, drop

and cower. *Take-CO-ver* they cantillate.
Whee-o, whee-o, high and low.

Juncos, pass to vireos. Catbirds steal the flow.
The chickadees have gone on lockdown.

They bore like bullets through the bleeding bark
of the cedars. Crows reload from rooftops.

II

House of Freaks

Come closer.
This is where I get to be the person
I am. Odd and unnumbered.
My kitchen teeth. My sponge tongue.
My paper doll skin. Here is where
I unwind the coil
of my hands and string my bare
face up like a lantern. Look,
we're like a family of road flares.
Did we get your attention? See,
I'm shedding my last pair
of eyes. I'm not watching
the parade of strangers.
We have cotton socks
and warm soup and the sound
of helicopters circling has finally
faded back into the everyday hum.
We've stopped reading the papers.
Now we make up the headlines
we want to hear. News flash:
a garden snail is crawling
across the flagstone outside.
There is a hole in the word *whole*
you can fall into, and if
you're not careful, your sentences
can backfire like a muscle car

on the interstate of your mouth.
But if you wipe your feet
and shut the door, you can
come in. Welcome home.

My Family

I used to keep old black and white photos in my wallet.
Just snapshots fished out of a shoebox at a junk store:

dark-eyed men in bomber jackets leaning against a pony car,
or sitting astride a tractor wearing khakis and an undershirt,

a pencil of mustache above their lip. Women with cat-eyed glasses,
dressed up in feathered hats for a night of gin rickeys,

arms draped across each other's shoulders and angling
for the camera. Even in grayscale I could see their cheeks

were rouged and their lips were slick with lipstick.
Sometimes I'd take the photos out and show them

to someone I'd just met. *This is my family*, I'd say,
and watch as they shuffled through the pile of strangers

politely noting how nice looking they were. It felt good
to know all anyone could ever know of me was what I was

willing to show them. This heavyset blonde posing
on the steps of a California bungalow wearing a fur coat

in the obvious heat of summer. These children splashing
in a kiddie pool on a lawn cluttered with beach balls

and hula hoops, a spray of water suspended mid-air
as the camera clicked on the girl's scream,

her brother's swashbuckling grin, their father watching
from a folding chair, a beaming fat baby on his lap.

I keep them ready, these people I don't know. *That's me*
I say, pointing at the fat baby. *I was happy then.*

Heroin

It is the dead center
of a hot, dry summer.
Every day we sit on the patio
and wait for the cool drafts
of evening. My daughter is crumpled
in a chair, her long legs folded
under her body, her arms wrapped
around herself as if she is cold.
I don't stop watching her.
It is the season of our addictions.

I want to think
we are in this together,
but she is in it alone
and I am just trying
to find some part of her,
a hand or a finger, even a lock
of her hair to grab hold of
to tow her safely past
the hard, biting edges
we are trying to live through.
Sometimes she gives me
a small, lovely smile
that I press into the hurt
I can't find a cure for.

In the evening
as the light grows sadder,
and the day no longer stings
we drive to the white church
where my daughter will say
her name to a roomful of strangers,
while I sit in the parking lot
waiting for her to come back
across the shimmering asphalt.

CT Scan

My son's brain
pulsates like a rare sea creature,
stunning in its complexity,
its near perfect symmetry.

The technician clicks through views
as if trying to find her way around
a topographic map. She pauses
to zoom in on a coral reef.

My son lies on the long white tongue
of the machine snapping up images,
his man-sized feet splay out to either side,
cleats untied; hands crossed over his chest.

His face is scored with the red lines
of the laser alignment system. Somewhere
in that luminous array of neurons
are his first words: *meow*, and *light*,

the way he puffs out his lower lip
when he's thinking or crinkles his eyes
when he's happy, his smile flaring
and dissipating like wood smoke.

Inside those folds are every conversation
we've ever had: tiger sharks and breathing trees,
and the time the tooth fairy didn't show —
both of us so astonished

she could forget. It's all there
in the axial and coronal views,
the stately cerebral cortex,
the stalwart cerebellum,

all three pounds of buckled gray matter
harboring his every evanescent thought,
what he remembers.
The secrets he keeps.

The Game

I love you I say to the boy. He's three.
I love you more, he says back. *But I love you most,*
I say and wonder how love became a competition.
I love you more than Halloween candy, I say.
I love you more than sky, he shouts. *I love you so much*
I must dance around the house all night, doing this, and I demonstrate
the move, which looks something like pitching a baseball with both hands
while shaking my ass. He looks impressed, comes back with *I love you*
fifty bonks on the head, and slaps the back of his own noggin again and again
to show me what this kind of love looks like. *I love you the whole driveway*
and parking lot. I love you every pothole in New York City. I love you
more than abcdefg. I love you more than purple, more than gold.
I love you more than cat vomit and dog poop. I love you all the dead people
in the cemetery. I love you eyeballs and bones and rotting skin, and . . . and . . .
he's looking around wildly for the right thing to say, his eyes scanning
the floor, the ceiling, the shelves, and then... *I love you so much*
I hate you. We stare at each other across the kitchen.
I know what he means. *I love you so much*
I hate you too.

The Scientist's Daughter

I have carried it with me, the morning
at the Kansas City Farmers' Market
when my father and I stood in front of a stall
where a man sold pork belly, ham hocks, fatback —
things we didn't eat.

In the bed of his trailer was a sleeping sow,
her face whiskered and wrinkled
like a tired old lady. My father, observant
and curious, coaxed me closer
to see the row of tiny pink piglets
tugging at her teats.

I was my father's daughter.
I didn't play with girl things, and yet,
I wanted to gather those babies up
and snuggle their bodies to mine.

But my father's gaze had turned
to the pig farmer, an obese man sitting on a stool
frying bacon in an electric skillet, a pile of rashers
stacked on a plate beside him. As he ate,
grease dripped onto his hands and chin.

The man saw my father watching, and paused
to press a dishrag against the oily folds of his neck.

The air was thick with the smell of pigs
and manure and frying. I wanted to walk away,
but my father's hands were on my shoulders.

My father, a man who moved through the world
as if everything was on display for his amusement,
and he was my tour guide to the exhibition.

I didn't think of him as unkind.
When he walked me through Skid Row,
he called the men by name, brought them coats
and socks, bought them hot meals. And yet,

I heard his remark before it arrived,
anticipated it like the hiss
of water hitting a hot pan.

Look, honey, a fat man eating bacon.

He said it as though his words were a gift
he was delighted to give me. He said it
so loud the air curled up and died around us.

The man stopped chewing and his hand froze
as though he was a conductor
holding a fermata
with a baton of burnt meat.

My father walked on. I stood there,
my cheeks flushing, my mouth dry.

The man's face gentled and he offered me
a small nod. I remember it
as a kind of welcome, my first introduction
to the exquisite sadness of shame.

Baby Facing the Wrong Way at the County Jail

A woman enters the waiting room
carrying a baby strapped into a car seat.
She sets him down so he is facing me.
Tucked under a heavy blanket, all I can see
is the round disc of his face.
Behind his pacifier, the edges of his mouth
flicker. I know he's smiling because of the pleats
around his eyes. I smile back and he smiles bigger.
He's a happy baby. *How old is he?*
I ask the woman who is reading a magazine
and seems to have forgotten
the baby at my feet. She looks up and I watch
her mind chew through my question.
Seven months maybe. Or eight, she says
then adds, *He isn't my baby.*
So, whose baby are you? I wonder.
I work for the state. I bring him here
to visit his father, the woman says
as the baby continues to smile
at the metal detector, the linoleum,
the folding chairs, the fluorescent lights shining
on everything ugly in that room.

Growing Apples in the County Jail

There is big excitement in C block today.
On the windowsill,
in a plastic ice cream cup,
a little plant is growing.
This is all the men want to talk about:
how an apple seed germinated
in a crack of damp concrete;
how they tore open tea bags
to collect the leaves, leached them in water,
then laid the sprout onto the bed
made of Lipton. How this finger
of spring dug one delicate root down
into the dark fannings and now,
two small sleeves of green
are pushing out from the emerging tip.
The men are tipsy with this miracle.
Each morning, one by one,
they go to the window and check
the progress of the struggling plant.
All through the day they return
to stand over the seedling
and whisper.

Lost

A boy who was lost in the woods says a bear kept him company.
No one can prove it didn't happen. —CNN

The bear felt the boy before she heard him,
sensed a disturbance deep in the knotweed,
and knew something was scared there.
At first, it unnerved her, but its cub-like crying
drew her closer, till a shift of wind
brought the unnatural smell
she'd learned to fear. She hesitated,
sniffed again. This was different.
Not so manlike or musky, it was nuanced
with sugar and sour milk.
She was cub-less that winter,
and drawn toward the hurt animal,
not with a hunger, but an ache.
The orphan had curled up
like a pup — nose to knees, whimpering.
She padded in, snuffing softly,
singing a lullaby of grunts and chuffs.
The child turned toward her musty breath,
reached his numb fingers out for her coarse coat.
She curled in her claws and lay down slowly,
settled herself so she wouldn't crush him,
made her body into a cradle,
and tucked him into her. He dozed.
She stayed, that night and the next

as the temperature dropped below freezing.
He told her his stories — purple crayons,
night kitchens, magic pebbles.
She clicked her tongue and hummed
about meltwater and spring. When she heard
the far-off calls growing closer,
she licked the fringe of blond fur
on his forehead, nudged him awake, and left.
Back in the fold of his family, they noticed
his unwavering gaze, the way he hesitated
in doorways, grazing the air with his face,
scenting the room, as if always searching
for something he'd lost.

Nancyland: A Visitor's Guide

Take care not to disturb the remains
of sleeping creatures when rummaging

through leaf litter and fallen branches,
especially near a riverbed or grave.

Empty your pockets as you walk.
It won't help you find your way,

but the birds will notice
and learn to listen for your steps.

Teach yourself the language of stones
and oceans. Open the windows

of your bones so the requiem
the trees sing when they sway

can enter. When the wind grows still,
and the hills begin to shiver, notice how

colors turn otherworldly before they fade
into the dusk they came from.

Hold the silence in your mind until it turns
into words. When the restless chair,

salvaged from your grandmother's barn,
calls you to the table, give thanks

for the patience of paper and the good pen
breathing between your fingers. Don't

answer the door for blood or money.
When you're done writing the poem,

put it back where you found it, buried
in the potter's clay of the past.

At night when you lie down, give thanks
for the soft, comforting stutter

of rain on the roof. Tell yourself,
If I lived here, I'd be home now.

Leopard Eats Meditating Monk

Forest officials said they had warned the monks against going too far.
—BBC NEWS

The leopard entered,
stood at the rim of thought
and waited. The monk still
had work to do. He was in love
with the way the light played
off the rose-colored canopy
of branches above him.
It was the beginning
of the dry season. Teak trees
were shedding their leaves
and all around, clusters
of tear-shaped drupes
fell to the forest floor.

Weeks passed; the monk detached
from the name his mother gave him.
He sat with wild boar
and barking deer, his back
resting against the buttressed trunk.
He knew inside the scaly bark
lay the deep-dark gold
of the heartwood.
He closed his eyes, imagined
his own heart beating in sync

and slowed the blood
in his veins to match
the unhurried flow.

The leopard stepped in.
Rested a reverent paw
against the monk's cheek.
The monk gazed into the devout
amber eyes. The leopard saw
no anger or greed
in the holy man's face.
This is my treasure, he thought.
As the leopard ate,
they shared between them,
not a single doubt.

Sanctuary

During the last years of her life
my mother developed the idea
that by touching her forehead to mine,
no one else could hear what she was saying.
I called it our Zone of Silence.
How funny to think the woman
standing next to us couldn't hear
my mother say, *that poor lady*
cried her mascara down to her chin,
or that she'd been giving her Vicodin
to the med tech who had broken
his pinky finger. Still, there was comfort
in this newly discovered level of indiscretion.
When she motioned me to come near,
I never knew what would spill forth.
Mostly, I was charmed to have her share
her secrets in this unlikely way, as if
joining our foreheads together
created a connection, and our closeness
gave whatever truth tumbled into the world
a sacred place on which to land.

Domain

I remember, as a child, discovering my body.
So many unique places, the odd topography
of my tongue with its spongey fungiforms
and papillae. The tremulous frenulum.

Those bowstrings inside my elbows.
That strange skull-shaped cap swimming above
the watery gap of my knee. I loved the way
my ears hid themselves like utility shelves

behind my hair, how conveniently they served
to keep it out of my eyes, my own auspiciously placed
drapery hooks. I remember being fascinated
with the way my fingertips could feel

both the touching and the part of me that was
being touched. So many ambiguous chambers,
my half-in, half-out belly button, the amphibious skin
of my lip, the slick mucosa of my cheeks,

so like the lining of my vagina, that private place
of intrigue, and maybe, a little shame.
But that was before I grew to know my body better,
and became so grateful I didn't have a penis —

that ungainly appendage. How I loved discovering
the noises I could make with the back of my throat
the pharyngeal clicks and whistles. All the hours
I spent practicing the manipulative instrument

of my mouth. There were smells too that I explored —
the scent of seawater clinging to my skin
on hot a day, the smell of blood
from a scraped knuckle, and the taste,

licked fresh from a cut, the tang of iron
and rust. Every part fair game in the mapping
of my bones and nerves, the muscles straining
to hold up this mysterious house. Even at this age,

I'm fascinated by the expanding realm of flesh
on my belly, springy and pinchable. Sunspots
shaped like Rorschach blots, black clouds
and winged creatures. Ruby-colored constellations

of angiomas. Crow's feet and cackle lines.
The foundation of my face settling in
for the long haul, each year my body becoming
more and more familiar.

Childhood Insomnia

I was the child terrified of time.
If I sat still, it ticked, and I hated the sound
of everything elapsing. During the day
I kept myself moving. At night, stupid with fear,
I'd lie in my bed and count,

    staring into the darkness worried
what the hours would do
if I wasn't awake to witness them.

The stakes were unbearable —
everyone I loved would grow old
and die. Each night I'd fight
    to keep from falling
       off the unsteady ledge of consciousness.
Instead, I'd roam the house
tapping on walls.

How weary I was: little shroud-weaver,
unknitting the nights. And every time
  I tripped into the abyss
I'd come back gasping
from all that nothingness.
      How hard it was to climb out
of silence, and later,
         the gut-punch

of waking up
knowing I'd lost those hours forever.

But I found out how to make time
mine. I spoke in unfinished sentences,
    repeated words in my head:
flabbergast, mollycoddle, kick the stick.

I carried rocks in my pockets:
    polished pebbles and ice stones,
my fingers memorizing their contours
and curves while I studied how to navigate
the day-lit world:
    staring at water stains
until they made sense, watching
my face age in mirrors. Listening,
        for the trees to exhale.

I taught myself to slip
in and out
of dreams, learned to open
        one second and savor
        the mysterious
kernels galloping on my tongue,
the talismanic syllables

sliding into the world.
        Then a glass could be emptied
and nothing bad happened.
Tangled string was just string.

But sometimes the unsleeping child creeps back.
    I look out through her tired eyes
and remember the moving shadows
of tables and chairs, the uncanny
call of the mockingbird,
        the devastating scent
of the night-blooming jasmine.

III

An Inventory of Inconsolable Objects

1. The disarticulated skeleton of a barn owl. 2. A bowl of doorknobs.
3. Seven antique mirrors, black spidery clouds drifting across
their de-silvered backs. 4. An old violin, body charred and broken,
seams split, pegbox cracked in half. 5. Dismantled clocks, moon dials
and click springs, hands and faces endlessly counting. 6. The bare arms
and necks of stripped chandeliers, still longing for their crystal teardrops
and coffin stones. 7. Cobalt apothecary jars, mouths caked with residue.
8. Two chairs, each missing a leg, what's left of a set. 9. A pair
of worn snakeskin cowboy boots, soles crusted with manure and mud.
10. Three fetal mice floating in a snow globe filled with formaldehyde
and glitter, their tiny feet almost human.

Confession

I laid the baby gophers onto the lid of a shoebox.
Hairless and blind, still fetal. Tiny pink apostrophes
with mouths rooting for milk. Tissue paper skin
so translucent you could see the dark nub

of each heart beating as every intake
of breath swelled through their bellies
in a convulsive shudder. Their nest destroyed.
Their mother's way back to the double-dug garden

wired shut. Still, I might have saved them.
But already their finger-buds were blossoming
into claws, the seeds of razor-teeth sprouting
in the upper jaw. Each thumbnail-sized pup

quivered with an ambition to live. I carried them
into the woods on their cardboard bier, noses and legs
twitching, as they dug through their last dream
of endless dirt and darkness.

The Thief

He didn't take the binoculars
or sunglasses. Left the Swiss Army knife
and owner's manual on the floor.
He didn't even steal the roll of quarters
I keep in the console. What he did take
was the small, spiral-bound notebook
filled with poems I'd scrawled
while stopped at intersections
or pulled over on the side of the road.

Now, I wake at night,
his eyes on mine, as if torn
from a magazine and taped over my own
so the world appears to me
through his widened sight.
There I am, rummaging through cars
trying to discover the story
that will save me: an apology,
or a prayer, one word that can click
me open like a switchblade.

Now, I'm growing
a second mouth. I'm learning
the language of asphalt
and shattered glass, feeling around
the dashboard with my new tongue.
I never knew there were so many ways

to describe darkness. Now I'm the person
running through shadows looking
for a rope, a bell, a harness, a fix
of meaning, terrified
of what I might find.

Unsolicited

She's sitting in a crowded subway car, zipping through email messages
on her phone and minding her own business when it appears:
a photo of a man's penis. —CNN

The first pic was blurry, so she might not have been sure. But
the second one should have resolved all doubt. His hand grasping it

so she could see the half-moons of his cuticles frowning
below the pale crown of flesh. Now the woman is glancing around.

She's wearing a pea coat over jeans though he imagines her naked,
her breasts swaying slightly as the car rocks back and forth. He didn't expect

what came next. She stood, furiously tossed her bob of hair, held up her phone
and said, *Is this yours?* She waved it around so others could see. *Is this yours?*

she said to the man seated next to him. *Is it yours?* she said to another man.
Look, she said, and then she shoved her phone into his face and said,

Is this yours? It seemed so absurd on the small face of her phone, under it,
the innocent airdrop request, "Steven's phone would like to share."

Are you Steven? She asked. The man next to him glanced over and said,
Not me. Wrong color, and for a moment, the two smiled over the joke.

He wondered if everyone could see his white cheeks turning shades of fire.
This wasn't what he'd intended. He thought she'd feel a flurry of curiosity,

perhaps a flush of desire. He is, after all, not a bad looking man, the kind
that walks comfortably through a locker room. He imagined she'd look around

uneasy, maybe edge her way to the exit doors to escape with his secret
stowed in her purse. He imagined she'd think of him at night, take it out

when she was alone and gaze at the soft, vulnerable skin of the glans,
the slightly erect shaft cupped in his palm, the mat of blonde hair. He didn't expect

all the commotion: a lady towing her small daughter to the far end of the car,
the man to his right chuckling, shaking his head, and the woman in front of him,

her voice a glass shattering, over and over, as if he was a dog who had soiled the carpet,
Is this yours? Is this yours? Is this yours?

Vengeance

"Do you smell shit?" my husband asked,
his face probing the air like a deer. Head turning
from side to side, nostrils flaring as he buttoned up.
He'd already showered, shaved. Was blow-dried —
had applied deodorant and cologne.

"What do you mean?" I asked.

Later I would have the locks changed, and
the credit cards cut. All the accounts closed.
But this night I just wanted to have fun —
to send him off gift-wrapped
in the aromas of home.

I'd fished a diaper from the dirty bin,
harvested some of the yellow and brown,
kneaded it beneath the collar, massaged some
under the label, carefully toothbrushed
a bit into the seams. It blended like a dream
into the deep blue hue of the fabric.
All this for the woman I wasn't
supposed to know about.

Gathering up his jacket and keys,
he leaned over to where I was
propped on pillows nursing the baby

and gave me a small kiss —
an obligatory deposit
into the bank of our marriage.

But that wonderful smell
trailed behind him, my blessing
as he walked off into the night.

Past Life

In a dive down the street
of a town I no longer call home,
I drank myself into another story,
one where I wasn't kissing hunters
whose names I didn't know —
lonely men who smelled
of wet fur and whisky.
In this new life you won't find me
sick on the sidewalk, wondering
where all my friends have gone
as the hesitant shadows of strangers
stroll by the drunk girl crouched
near an alley in front of a bar
pulsing with bodies, thinking,
you poor fucked up thing,
gravel and broken glass
cutting into her hands and knees
as she held her head down like a barn animal
and the bullion of beer and bile poured
from her mouth to pool in the gutter,
the streetlight reflecting
on the wet pavement, its beautiful,
moon-shaped yellow.

Self Portrait as Sea Slug

It's cold science.

Some can self-decapitate
and grow a new body.
         But not all can manage it.

It takes guts to carry on without your vital parts.

Camper vans and carving knives.
Play dates and block parties.
The Gibson guitar we bought at a pawn shop.

After, I was just hunger and mouth,
    eating my way through time
         without taste or pleasure.

         I bathed myself in distance.
    All I wanted
was to forget

         the memories blinking on and off
in my severed head.

    My abandoned body guttering, growing cold.

It wasn't easy to let my past die.

All those years spent moving
                further and further into

the life I would cut myself off from:

                my ex with his raging face.
            His burled skin and incoherent hands.

The relentless hammering of my frightened heart.

But when the dread of another hour
                tethered into the body tethered to him
grew too heavy, I did what had to be done.
            I pulled along the perforated line,

beheaded myself neatly.

It was an act of survival. Sometimes
there is no plan B.

But the headless corpus still moves,
still wants to be touched.

On the eleventh day of my disembodiment,
            an elongated ache began to pulse
in the place beneath where my left breast

once was, while the gaping wound
            at the nape of my amputated past
                slowly stitched itself together

and the pain became iridescent,
        a rhythmic quiver,
and began, once again, to beat.

To the Jewish Girl Praising Jesus in the Gospel Choir After Her Parents' Divorce

Here's to the child who walked herself into the Holy Spirit
      Church of Christ to eighty-six her sorrows in a crucible

of music. Daughter, embracing the sound of fire, found
      herself a fortress of voices raised in praise. Found herself

sheltered on the far left of the first row, her hands held
      to the sky, pounding the floor with her feet in a resounding

kiss-my-ass to the Palisades ladies who didn't want
      the Jewish child singing in the Christian choir. But, O

that Sephardic dark-haired angel, her mouth stretched
      wide enough to swallow the stars, there on stage, her eyes

rejoicing, carried away by the intoxicating rock and sway
      of rapture. O little one busting out the Bible

stomp, released from grief through Glory
      in Excelsis, the latchkey kid finding her mojo

singing hymns in the name of Him. O, praise that girl
      standing on toes, her face reposed, tossed and lost

and put back together by the heavenly shovels
      and holy-rolling bones of the Jesus beat.

Heavens to Betsy

My mother spoke in idioms and expletives.
When she said she was beside herself,
I pictured two of her standing next to one another,
each equally perplexed by the other's presence.
Hell's bells conjured images of a church
in perpetual flames. When the toast burnt
or milk spilt she would call out a cathartic
Jesus H. Christ, which made me think of my father
whose middle name was Howard, a logical leap
because I'd been told Jesus was also a Jew.
Once she said she'd had it up to *here*
and I imagined her on a boat floating away,
her annoyance finally rising high enough
to cast off from the everyday drama of us.
Good grief confused me. How could grief
ever be good? But *Christ on a bike*
made me smile, a grown-up riding a tricycle,
his flowing robes gathered so he could pump
the tiny pedals with his oversized feet.
Holy Mary Mother of God!
Such a comforting mouthful.
Christ on a cracker, Geez Louise, Holy moly
(who even knows what a moly is).
And because I was a literal-minded child,
I spent many years hoping I'd get to meet

Betsy, a distant relative of my mother's —
the lucky woman (unlike us)
slated to inherit heaven.

Supernova

After my mother died,
I spent the day packing her things.
Tiffany birds, tiny Limoges boxes,
her favorite blue blouse. Now, there is
nothing left but vacant rooms.
My son and I go outside to look at the sky.
Between the bowl of the Big Dipper
and the North Star a violent explosion
millions of years ago has just become
visible to astronomers on earth,
though we can't see it with our naked eyes.
Even so, we lie on the lawn
and look up into a black pool
pinpricked by millions of needles of light.
I am floating facedown into emptiness
when the voice of my young son
fills the darkness. "Did you know,
all the atoms in our bodies
were once inside a star?"
He leans his head against mine.
I breathe in earth and grass
and the cool, damp air.
My heart is too small
to hold this night.

George the Snail, Believed to Be the Last of His Species, Dies in Hawaii

. . . he lived his last days alone in a terrarium . . . alongside an ample supply of fungi . . . —THE NEW YORK TIMES

This is a survivor story
that doesn't end well.
George, the last Hawaiian mollusk,
Achatinella apexfulva, is dead.
He/She/They enjoyed a last supper of fungi
in a lonely climate-controlled terrarium,
and then succumbed to old age.
Keepers had searched in vain for a mate
with whom George could procreate.
They dreamed of babies with tiny shells
twisted like vanilla and chocolate soft serve.
But all kin had fallen prey to pathogens,
drier habitats, and the voracious appetite
of the rosy wolfsnail, an invasive predator
(introduced by you-know-who) that is eating
the native snails into extinction. So,
another species on the missing list.
One small death, another final loss.
Disappearing next: the South China tiger,
or the elusive vaquita gulf porpoise,
and after that, perhaps, the northern bald ibis.
Pundits tout the potential silver lining
in George's demise: increased awareness

of global crisis. I think mostly
we don't notice. There's too much
to take in. Glaciers calving ice floes
the size of Manhattan. Rivers evaporating.
Commuters wearing gas masks.
And in Syria, a starving child, so frail
the paper tape holding her feeding tube
tears her skin. When she dies
her loved ones will carry
their sadness forward
into their own deaths.
The clouds are already heavy
with our absence.

Ode to the Non-Conformist

Evidence is mounting that a tiny subatomic particle seems to be disobeying the known laws of physics —THE NEW YORK TIMES

Tiny lepton, tatted head to toe,
        sporting a leather jacket and a Harley,
                waving its middle finger at physics

as it faces down the four fundamental forces
        of nature with a cocksure *fuck you* to all
                the milquetoast particles who get star struck

and giddy when this punk morsel
        stage dives into the mosh pit of relativity
                and breaks all the cosmic laws

slam dancing to its own subatomic trance mix.
        Even when accelerated, smashed and fat-shamed,
                this "overweight electron" continues to mock

an international team of 200 scientists
        with its too-cool-for-school behavior.
                When the laws of physics mandate that it spin,

                it does the opposite. Some say this rebel
        might hold the key to the mysteries
that have long preoccupied our lonely species.

Some say it carries the secrets of dark matter
        in the confines of its supercharged soul, and
                they intend to torture a confession

out of this infinitesimal insurgent. So they place its bad-ass
        onto a giant track and make it run
                through a superconducting circus act

at minus 450 degrees to study its peculiar wobble.
        O puny humans. They are no match.
                I cheer for the muon.

Keep silent, little one.
        Hold onto your secrets, even if
                the entire universe hangs in the balance.

Still

The last apple hangs on into winter.
Shriveled and brown as a shrunken head,
it holds onto the branch even while falling
further into itself. Drops of rain-sweat
slide down its mottled skin,
catch light from the sun and turn gold.

Isn't persistence beautiful?

The woman who shows up daily
for her dose of methadone.
The man punching the clock shift after shift
though he carries his heart through each day
in a cold, empty chest. The small boy
who tries to make sense of the lines
his teacher has made on the chalkboard.

How do we keep on?

The bird drops its song, over and over,
picking it up and dropping it,
little notes spilling down the mountain.

My father on his deathbed, eyes still filled
with wonder, he lingers longer and longer

in the space between each breath,
stepping carefully onto the ledge
of his last thought.

Why I Tie My Hair to Trees

Thick, black handfuls gathered
from the comb. I carry the nest of it
outside to drape on a low-hanging branch
of the oak. Later when I look, it's gone,
carried off by wind or birds.
I like to imagine it as home
for song sparrows, the strands
woven into the twigs and leaves.
Or collected by wood rats
along with cobwebs and cloth
and buried in the woodpile,
a piece of me nestled into the lives
of these creatures. Or maybe,
blown into the trees, tangled
in the lacy crown of the hemlock.
At night, when the outlines
of familiar objects run into the dark,
I like to think there is a part of me
that isn't afraid, one slender curl
shining in the moonlight.

Notes

The Poem "Tilt-A-Whirl" is dedicated to my sister Janis. Special thanks to Tracy K. Smith and David Lehman for choosing this poem for *Best American Poetry*. That was so much better than winning a pony!

The quote, "youth is nothing but sadness... and longing," at the beginning of the Poem "Kansas" is from an essay entitled, "A Diamond to Cut" by Dawn Powell published in *The New Yorker*, June 26, 1995.

A line in the poem "Kansas" was changed after Sharon Olds misheard the word "purring" as "purling" at a reading following a workshop with her and Naomi Shihab Nye. "Did you say, 'the purling throat of God'?" she asked, and because I was star struck, I nodded yes. "That's wonderful" she said. Of course, I immediately changed the word purring to purling. Thank you, Sharon.

The poem, "The Invisible Mother" is based on the genre of Hidden Mother photography common in the Victorian Era in which young children were photographed with their mother present but hidden in the photograph. "The Hidden Mother" by Linda Fregni Nagler is a haunting coffee table collection of these photographs.

The epigraph in the poem "Missing History," is a quote from *The New York Times* article by Sharon Attia published on March 29, 2019.

The quote that appears as an epigraph in the poem "The Road" is from the *LA Times* article by Nabih Bulos entitled "Raining rockets, scattered corpses, an existential battle: A 500-mile journey across a week of war" published March 5, 2022. The poem is a reverent nod to Bridget Pegeen Kelly's poem "Song," and Wallace Steven's poem, "The Snow Man."

Special thanks to Kaveh Akbar and Jeb Livingston for choosing the poem "Siren Song" to appear in *Best New Poets* 2021. The Epigraph is from an article by Michelle Lim entitled "Australian magpie mimics emergency sirens as deadly fires rage," published on CNN January 2, 2020.

The Poem "CT Scan" is dedicated to Jonah. The tooth fairy sends her apologies.

The Poem "The Game" is dedicated to Atlas, who I love more than all the poop in the Universe.

"Growing Apples" in the County Jail is dedicated to the incarcerated persons who participate in the poetry workshops at the Santa Cruz County Jail. For more information please go to: www.poetryinthejails.org

The epigraph for the poem "Lost" is the title of an article on CNN by Amir Vera and Samira Said published on January 29, 2019

The epigraph for the poem "Leopard Eats Meditating Monk" is from an article on BBC.com posted on December 13, 2018

The poem "The Thief "is dedicated to whoever rummaged through my car one night in Oakland. I am grateful you didn't take my birding binoculars. I hope you are enjoying the poems.

The epigraph for the poem "Unsolicited" is from an article written by Doug Criss published on CNN on February 10, 2019.

The Poem "Self Portrait as Sea Slug," is based on a study lead by author Sayaka Mitoh of Nara Women's University in Japan who observed sea slugs self-decapitating and then regenerating new bodies.

The title of the poem "George the Snail, Believed to Be the Last of His Species . . . Dies in Hawaii," is from the title of an article written by Julia Jacobs in *The New York Times* on January 10, 2019. The epigraph is a quote from the same article.

The epigraph of the poem "Ode to the Non-Conformist," is from an article written by Dennis Overbye in *The New York Times* on April, 27, 2021.

Acknowledgments

Acknowledgment is made to the editors of the journals in which the following poems appeared:

Prairie Schooner: "The Game," and "CT Scan"

TriQuarterly: "The Road"

Alaska Quarterly Review: "House of Freaks"

The Adroit Journal: "Coachwhip"

The Hopkins Review: "Leopard Eats Meditating Monk"

New Ohio Review: "Tilt-A-Whirl," "Siren Song," My Family,"

Rattle: "Still," "How Are We Doing," "Supernova," "Crescent Moon," (as "Deadbeat"), "Resurrection," and "How to Forget"

The Rumpus: "Unsolicited"

Massachusetts Review: "Snapshot," (as "My First Grade Picture")

River Styx: "Vengeance"

Catamaran: "Why I Tie My Hair to Trees"

Nimrod: "We All Fall Down"

"Tilt-A-Whirl," was selected by Tracy K. Smith for *Best American Poetry* 2021 and received a *Pushcart Prize* special mention in the 2023 edition.

"Siren Song," was selected by Kaveh Akbar for *Best New Poets* 2021.

"Growing Apples in the County Jail" appeared in *American Life in Poetry* and in the anthology, *How to Love the World: Poems of Gratitude and Hope* edited by James Crews, and in *Punishment*, a Rattle Chapbook Series selection (as "Growing Apples"). It also appears in *That's a Pretty Thing to Call It*, Prose and Poetry by Artists Teaching in Carceral Institutions edited by Leigh Sugar.

"Baby Facing the Wrong Way in the County Jail" appeared in "Punishment,"
a Rattle Chapbook Series selection.

Gratitude

To KMA Sullivan for giving this manuscript a home and bringing it to print. I am honored to be pressmates with the amazing authors and poets of YesYes Books. To KMA and Gale Thompson for their insightful notes and editorial guidance. The poems and manuscript were greatly enriched by your thoughtful suggestions and counsel. To Alban Fisher for his designs. To Alexandra Gallagher for her art.

For my beloved sisters in poetry who patiently and lovingly helped shape these poems through many drafts: Jamaica Baldwin, Michele Bombardier, Farnaz Fatima, Veronica Kornberg, Amanda Moore, Julie Murphy, Dion O'Reilly, Rebecca Patrascu, Emily Ransdell, Erin Redfern, Jennifer Saunders, Emily Sernaker, and Cynthia White. And for Craig van Rooyan, a poetry sister in all but gender.

For my dear Friday writing buddies: Ali, Victoria, and Laurie (the best bar-writing partner a gal could ever hope to have).

For all my fellow volunteers in the Poetry in the Jails Project, especially Renee and Deb who keep it going and for Ellen who co-founded the program with me.

To the women and men in the Santa Cruz County Jails and the kids at the Juvenile Hall who bravely show up every week to put words on the page and who carry the transformative power of poetry back into the community and their lives.

So much gratitude for my teachers in the MFA program at Pacific University: To the late Marvin Bell who taught me the poetry should continue even after the poem ends. To Joe Millar who taught me to get out of my head and just write some fucking poems. To Kwame Dawes, Frank Gaspar, and Danusha Lameris for encouragement and guidance. To Dorianne Laux who helped me discover the treasure trove of "weird Americana" poems lurking untapped in my metaphorical attic and for being the bad-ass of poetry we all want to be when we grow up.

To Patricia Smith for spending time with this collection and for her generous and thoughtful words of praise. I am forever grateful.

Enduring gratitude to Ellen Bass — teacher, mentor, and steadfast friend. Thank you for your immeasurable support and guidance. My writing is indelibly stitched with everything you've taught me.

For all the writers with whom I shared time and space in Ellen's Wednesday workshop.

To the poetry editors who gave my poems a home in their journals and offered encouragement and notes. Especially Dave Wanzyck, Dora Malech, Tim Green, Daniel Fliegel, Peter LaBerge, Lesley Wheeler, and Suzanne Paola Antonetta. To Tracy K. Smith and David Lehman. To Kaveh Akbar and Jeb Livingston. Your acceptances helped keep the dogs of self-doubt at bay.

Endless gratitude to Alan Fox, dearest friend and co-conspirator. The Patron Saint of Poetry. Do we dare disturb the Universe? It was an auspicious day when we met in a writing workshop at USC. And for the beautiful Daveen, who is always taking care of the world.

To my family, who won't stop making fun of the way I say "sandwich." For every sobremesa spent in their company. For their infinite love and support and for an endless wellspring of inspiration. To my daughter-in-law, Lindsay Miller, for her keen eye and feedback. And always to my daughter, Tamara Miller, fellow poet, brightest heart, my most ferocious supporter.

To my grandmother Babette who passed down the poetry gene through her DNA. To my children and grandchildren to whom I bequeath it. May your words heal this beautiful, broken world.

To all the women whose stories were never told.

Also from YesYes Books

Born Backwards by Tanya Olson

Stay by Tanya Olson

a falling knife has no handle by Emily O'Neill

Another Way to Split Water by Alycia Pirmohamed

To Love An Island by Ana Portnoy Brimmer

Tell This to the Universe by Katie Prince

One God at a Time by Meghan Privitello

I'm So Fine: A List of Famous Men & What I Had On by Khadijah Queen

If the Future Is a Fetish by Sarah Sgro

Gilt by Raena Shirali

Say It Hurts by Lisa Summe

Boat Burned by Kelly Grace Thomas

Helen Or My Hunger by Gale Marie Thompson

As She Appears by Shelley Wong

RECENT CHAPBOOK COLLECTIONS

Vinyl 45s

 Inside My Electric City by Caylin Capra-Thomas

 Exit Pastoral by Aidan Forster

 Of Darkness and Tumbling by Mónica Gomery

 Crown for the Girl Inside by Lisa Low

 Juned by Jenn Marie Nunes

 Scavenger by Jessica Lynn Suchon

 Unmonstrous by John Allen Taylor

 Preparing the Body by Norma Liliana Valdez

 Giantess by Emily Vizzo

Blue Note Editions

 Kissing Caskets by Mahogany L. Browne

 One Above One Below: Positions & Lamentations by Gala Mukomolova

 The Porch (As Sanctuary) by Jae Nichelle